DEAN JONES' CRICKET TIPS

Dean Jones played 52 Tests for Australia between 1984 and 1992, scoring 3,631 runs at an average of 46.55, and making 11 centuries. He also played in 164 one-day internationals for Australia between 1984 and 1994, scoring 6,068 runs at an average of 44.61, including seven centuries.

All up, he played 245 first-class matches, scoring 19,188 runs at an average of 51.85, including 55 centuries.

Dean Jones was a pivotal member of some of Australia's greatest cricket teams, including the 1987 World Cup-winning team, and the 1989 Ashes-winning team. His 210 in stifling heat at Chennai in 1986 is regarded as one of the best innings ever played, and through the early 1990s he was widely regarded as the best one-day batsman in the world.

He is one of Victoria's greatest-ever cricketers, and captained the state. He is currently the coach of Islamabad United in the Pakistan T20 league, and commentates on cricket for Star Sports in India and for Macquarie Radio Network in Australia, and writes for Fairfax in Melbourne and Sydney.

With love to my three girls,
Jane, Gussie, and Phoebe

DEAN JONES' CRICKET TIPS

(the things they don't teach you at the Academy)

ILLUSTRATIONS BY JOHN SPOONER

SCRIBE
Melbourne • London

Scribe Publications
18–20 Edward St, Brunswick, Victoria 3065, Australia
2 John St, Clerkenwell, London, WC1N 2ES, United Kingdom

Published by Scribe 2016

Text copyright © Dean Jones 2016
Illustrations copyright © John Spooner 2016

Printed and bound in Australia by Opus Group

Scribe Publications is committed to the sustainable use of natural
resources and the use of paper products made responsibly from those
resources.

ISBN 9781925321838 (Australian edition)
ISBN 9781911344094 (UK edition)

CiP data entries for this title are available from the National Library of
Australia and the British Library.

scribepublications.com.au
scribepublications.co.uk

CONTENTS

INTRODUCTION

A LIFETIME'S WORTH OF 'ONE PERCENTERS'

This book has been quite a few years in the making, when I think about it. And I think about cricket ... a lot! I love the game. It's been my life, and as much as the game has changed, it stays the same in many ways, too.

I last played for Australia in the 1990s, but 20 years on I am lucky to remain involved in the game as a coach and a media commentator, right at its beating heart.

Islamabad United is my team, and we won the inaugural title of the Pakistan Super League T20 competition in Dubai in February 2016. What a moment that was for all of us! I hope we can repeat that success in 2017 and I get another ice-bucket shower. That is one ice bath that I love to take!

My television work for Star Sports takes me around the world, and allows me to keep in touch with all the great players of the modern game, as well as some of the legends of the recent past. Many of them, I am happy to say, are represented in this book.

The book has been bobbing around in my mind for a few years now. Watching young players, it occurred to me that while there is a huge amount of coaching nowadays, there is actually too much information rolling around in players' heads at times. If you look at players from, say, the under-12 level through to international cricket, they would possibly have up to 15 different coaches during that time. Fifteen, through the age levels—to representative cricket, to state or provincial level, and on to national level! And every single one of those coaches would have a different philosophy and would be wanting to do his thing.

Personally, the best three coaches that I had were my father, Barney, who was a fine player at top-level club cricket in Melbourne when I was a boy; Keith Stackpole, the former Australian

Test opening batsman; and Bob Simpson, who was coach of Australia when we had our great period in the late 1980s and 1990s. A lot of what they told me was old school. But old school still applies in the game today. If I was playing today, I would hire my own coach and take him everywhere so that I could draw upon him when I needed him, as players do in tennis and golf, for example.

A player has to filter all this information and make his or her own decisions, has to work out which part of what they're told applies to his or her game. That is a crucial part of becoming a good player. For instance, Chris Rogers, the recent Australian Test opener, came to me a couple of years ago because he had problems with playing spin. Rogers had played most of his cricket in Perth, where the ball bounces trampoline-style and everyone learns to play off the back foot, so playing on dry, turning decks was vastly different for him when he broke into the Aussie team. Graeme Swann, England's excellent off spinner, gave him nightmares.

Rogers sought my help at a time when he had already made more than 20,000 runs, which shows you how the game evolves and how every player needs to keep finding new ways of dealing with new problems. What I tried to get Chris to do was to believe in what I taught him, then to work it out himself — in other words, to take ownership of his thoughts and his game. In my view, that is the key to coaching: to help the player to help him- or herself.

It is a lot easier when you have played 20 years as a professional, but not so easy if you are starting out. When I look at modern cricketers, I really wonder whether they are being told about the 'one-percenters', the little tips that can take you from being good to great, or from average to good. That is the premise of this book: an exercise in finding the one-percenters. Because at the very top level of cricket, everyone has major talent, and at that point it becomes about how your brain functions. It is that space between your ears, it is about how well you understand your own game, understand the game itself, and how you work out what you can and cannot do.

The best example of how the little things work is Sachin Tendulkar, the greatest batsman of the modern era and one of the best ever. I watched him closely and studied his statistics, and worked out that he only scored from about 30 per cent of the deliveries that he faced; this tells me, as you're about to see, that defence is a primary weapon in batting — although it is not what they show on the highlight reels.

Yes, the game has changed, but it is still a contest between bat and ball. The players hit it further than they used to, and the tactics have been tweaked, but it has not changed as much as people think it has. Everything has been tried before, pretty much, when you think about teams going hard early in one-day internationals, which the Sri Lankans did with Sanath Jayasuriya and Romesh Kaluwitharana in the 1990s. Back then, the Australians did well when batting by holding on to their wickets until around the 30th over, and then accelerating, but Pakistan were doing the same to win the World Cup in 1992. Often, you will see what looks like a new method, but the truth is if you delve into the past it will have been tried before.

So this book is about one-percenters, and finding the edge. It is targeted at absolutely every cricketer, from eight-year-olds to internationals, boys and girls. I am thankful to John Spooner, the great journalist and illustrator who was with *The Age* newspaper in Melbourne for so many years, for providing the artwork. When I met John, I discovered that he was a cricket enthusiast who is still playing the game at an age that I am not about to mention here! Also, thanks to Martin Blake, a long-time friend and sports journalist, for doing the editing and getting involved in the project, as well as to Henry Rosenbloom, the founder and publisher of Scribe, who so warmly greeted the idea when we pitched it to him. We all found common ground in cricket, the beautiful game.

I am grateful to the dozens of great cricketers whom I badgered for a tip or two to put the cream on the cake of this book — from the immortal Sachin Tendulkar, to Wasim Akram, to Nathan Lyon, and to all the rest. Their contribution is immense.

I hope you enjoy it. I certainly loved putting it together.

Dean Jones

BATTING TIPS

STANCE: THE BOXER'S POSITION

I really don't care what stance a batsman has as long as he gets into a boxer's position at ball release. Think of the great Muhammad Ali's stance in the ring, his shoulders slightly open, head over the front foot, both eyes level, and his weight over the balls of his feet. This is so powerful a position that it allows any batsman to move forward or back, wherever the ball is pitched.

Now, there have been some irregular or unconventional stances, such as Shivnarine Chanderpaul's and Kepler Wessels'. Both batsmen were very successful, but they both got into a strong boxer's position when the bowler was about to release the ball. So I ask you, what position do you think you are in when the bowler releases the ball? If you're not in the boxer's, adjust your stance to allow your body to get into the right position.

THE BIGGEST MISTAKE

From under ten cricket up to Test matches and T20 internationals, the most common error that I see from batsmen is not watching the length. If you go forward to a ball that is too short, you will get hit. If you go back to a ball that is pitched up, you will get knocked over. In batting, we have only two options. You need to get that right.

When I was young, the former Australian Test batsman Lindsay Hassett gave me a tip on working out length. He put a piece of rope straight across the pitch, about three metres down. If the ball pitched shorter than the rope, I was to go back; if it was past the rope I went forward. Then I had to envisage that when I played in a game situation. Quite often, you can use a mark that is already on the pitch for a guideline.

YOUR BEST DEFENCE

I work on the 70–30 principle with batting, in that you should be defending or leaving 70 per cent of balls. I looked at Sachin Tendulkar, who made 50 Test centuries for India. Sachin averaged 180 balls faced for each of those centuries.

In order, his three most common shots while compiling those centuries were forward defence, back defence, and leaving the ball. That added up to 130 of those 180 balls he faced (72 per cent). This tells you something important.

You need to have a strong defence. If you have all three of the big defensive techniques —forward defence, back defence, and good leaving — you can average 50 in Test cricket, I believe. If you have two of them, and one is a strong forward defence, you can average 40. If you only have one of the three, you had better find another job.

And don't forget, the 30 per cent is crucial, too. That's offence, the shot-making ability.

PREMEDITATE YOUR MOVE

I believe the top batsmen in the world are (not necessarily in order): Virat Kohli of India, Steve Smith of Australia, AB de Villiers of South Africa, Joe Root of England, and Kane Williamson of New Zealand. The common denominator with that group is that they all look to go on the back foot early. In other words, as the bowler gets into his delivery stride, they have movements of varying degrees to the back foot.

Many of the greats in the past like Bradman, Harvey, Weekes, and others played off the back foot when given the chance. What this does is allow the batsmen to have more time to play the shot than prominent front-foot players. They invariably have more time and more options to play the ball to wherever they choose to hit it.

Most Australian kids learn to play on synthetic or matting wickets. This surface always makes the ball bounce more than it should, thus driving the ball is the hardest shot to play. The easiest shots are on the back foot as the surface provides a consistent bounce and it is far easier to play the hook, pull, and cut shots.

Therefore I implore most kids to get on the back foot as much as you can when playing on these pitches. I was a big front-foot player and if I started my career again, I would definitely have been a back-foot player.

BEING COMFORTABLE: SACHIN TENDULKAR

The mighty Sachin Tendulkar, scorer of more runs than any other player in Test and one-day international cricket, knew the value of finding a level of comfort at the crease. It is interesting and it is something that I raised with Sachin.

'To be a consistent run maker on all pitches around the world you need to adapt to the conditions and play the right strokes accordingly,' he told me. 'Also you don't feel the same every day, and sometimes I didn't feel comfortable at the crease. This feeling was probably around 15–20 per cent of the time when I batted.

'What I learned to do when feeling uncomfortable was to change my stance. Sometimes I would widen my stance and lower my centre of gravity to keep me more stable, and other times I would move around the crease, and this helped me for some reason to find balance at the bowler's ball release. Other times I might just open up with my front or left foot, where instead of pointing to cover point, it pointed towards extra cover.'

Sachin used the example of a 1997 Test match against South Africa at Newlands to illustrate his point. 'We were 29/3 after day two and I was not out one. In the morning with a net practice I felt so uncomfortable in my stance and my feet felt heavy, so to get them moving I thought of how Michael Slater would shuffle before the ball was bowled. So I practised this move with some throwdowns before play, and I felt a lot more at ease, and I went on to make 169 against the likes of Allan Donald, Shaun Pollock, and Brian McMillan.

'So if you don't feel right at the crease, be proactive and don't be scared to change your stance to give yourself a better feeling from within.'

SACHIN TENDULKAR

PLAYING SPIN

Don Bradman said the greatest player he saw play spin was the great Lindsay Hassett, who played for Australia in the 1930s, 1940s, and 1950s. He was so good that it was said he could have played the great leg spinner Bill O'Reilly with a pogo stick if required!

I got the chance to catch up with Lindsay before the 1986 tour to India, and I knew that I was going to play on turners against quality spin. So I asked him what his philosophy was when playing a spinner. Lindsay replied: 'You play them two ways. I always like to watch their flight and use my feet to hit them on the full or half volley. Or, if the ball is pitched short, I like to play them off the back foot. I never play a forward defence to them as that means they beat you in flight. If it's up above your eye line, get forward as far as you can. Otherwise play back! Now go get me a Scotch!'

When I returned with a Scotch, Lindsay asked me how far down the wicket I could go. I replied, 'about three metres'. Lindsay then said at practice to put a small thread of cotton across the pitch at the three-metre mark when facing the spinners, and if the bowler landed it in the

LINDSAY HASSETT

zone, then to be up on the Twinkle Toes and hit it on the full or half-volley. If the ball was pitched short of the cotton, play off the back foot.

This tip helped me enormously in India, and well beyond that. Even in Test matches, where I obviously could not take out my piece of cotton, I can remember looking for blemishes on the pitch three metres out so that I could work out whether to use my feet or not.

Trust me when I say this: spin bowlers DO NOT like you running at them. They say they do ... But they don't, I can assure you.

THE EYES HAVE IT

I recommend that batsmen find out which is their dominant eye. To do that, close one eye and look at a spot on a wall, or if necessary, go into a spectacle shop and ask them! It's not too hard.

Batsmen need to keep their eyes level in the set-up and stance. Ricky Ponting is a great example of this; his eyes were perfectly level as he prepared to play.

To make sure your eyes are level, line up the grille on your helmet with the sightscreen (if there is one in place), or a rooftop. Your right eye should be over the off stump in your stance, and

if someone took a snap of your head, it should fit in the nine inches directly over the three stumps.

SAFER GROUND: SACHIN TENDULKAR

India's maestro Sachin Tendulkar is the only man to have scored 100 international centuries, counting his Test and one-day international games, and he told me that he was an advocate of training how he played. Sachin felt that to mess around at practice was to invite bad habits to creep in. He also liked the idea that a ball struck on the ground could not be caught.

'I hated getting out anywhere, in a game, in the nets or in the streets when I was with my friends as a kid,' he told me. 'To be a consistent bowler or batsman you need to do the basics well. My coach when I was young was Ramakant Achrekar in Mumbai, a terrific coach who wanted me to hit the ball along the ground. He would often place a rupee on top of my off stump and had lots of fielders around the bat and I would have to play for 15–20 minutes without getting out. My reward, if I could manage to keep my wicket, was the rupee.

'This was great coaching for me to simulate the same pressures I would face in a game.

SACHIN TENDULKAR

Sir Donald Bradman only hit six sixes in his Test career, and that was by choice. The risk and reward for him was too much to risk his wicket. By trying to hit a six for an extra two runs, was it worth it? Why not hit it along the ground for four and be content. If Sir Donald played like that, why not me?

'So I was always taught to play straight early, build a platform in your innings, and hit the ball along the ground. I know it might sound boring to some, but the first 15–20 minutes to me was everything. Trying to look solid and sound gave no confidence to bowlers and fielders, and then I would go about my work and have some fun. I loved my coach's favourite motto for batting: "You watch the bowlers for the first 15 minutes and then the bowlers can watch you for the rest of the day!"'

AVOIDING THE BLOOD RUSH

A blood rush is when your gut instinct tells you to take on a bowler to hit him out of the park. On most occasions, this failed and every batsman has had a blood rush at some point.

I played competitive cricket from the time I was ten, and right from that time I fought with the blood rush. Luckily a batsman has two sensors advising him on what strategy he should employ while facing a certain bowler. One sensor is his gut instinct, the creativity within him, and how he wants to play a certain bowler. This gut instinct often got me into trouble as it always wanted me to smash a bowler to all parts.

The second sensor is what your brain or head is telling you. This instinct always wanted me to play the conservative or percentage way. It always said to me 'be patient'. My father, Barney, always said to me: 'Just bat for time.' And it made sense, because if I batted four hours, for instance, my natural ability would allow me to make a hundred.

Throughout my career, 90 per cent of the time those two sensors disagreed with each other. When this occurred, I was disciplined enough to follow the way my brain told me, BUT, here is the kicker ... if your head and your gut instinct both agree on what strategy you should employ next, then that's when the real fun starts!!

One day in a Sheffield Shield match against Tasmania I felt a massive blood rush coming while facing left-arm spinner Dan Marsh. So I stopped him while he was in his delivery stride and apologised profusely, saying that I'd had a notion that I wanted to hit him over the sightscreen. Everyone laughed and I went through my routine to face the next ball. Immediately, I danced down the pitch and proceeded to put him in the stands! I apologised and said: 'I can't help myself when you are bowling!'

FINDING GAPS

As a batsman, you will go through phases of hitting the ball to the field too often. It's a waste of time, and it just builds pressure upon you, so I recommend that you change something.

So either bat a step outside your crease, or change your guard. If you bat outside the crease, it changes the length for the bowler and it changes the angles that you hit to.

If you bat on leg stump, try moving your guard across to off stump, or vice versa. Again, the angles are changed, and you might unlock your shot-making. Plus, you will *feel* like you are doing something about it.

BAT PLANES AND SYNCHING

When a batsman is getting hit on the pads a lot, it means that his premeditative move is wrong and his front foot is getting in the way of his bat plane. I struggled with this a lot throughout my career, as did Shane Watson, the Australian all-rounder. This horrible feeling of your head falling to cover cost me many a run and badly affected my bat plane or the idea of playing straight.

My coach, Keith Stackpole, a former Test opener with Australia, gave me the best tip to solve this problem. Keith threw balls at me in the nets, but no matter where the ball pitched, I had to play it off the back foot and hit it straight out of the net. I found it gave me better balance.

The ball that was pitched full was always the hardest to hit. After ten minutes of this and then going back to my normal way, it definitely helped my balance and got my front foot out of the way.

I never liked the term that I hear: 'His footwork is brilliant.' Because your feet would not move if it was not for the proper movement of your head. I like to keep things simple when batting. Being in SYNCH is what batting is all about, and what I mean is this:

1. Get your HEAD to the PITCH OF THE BALL
2. Then place your foot to the pitch of the ball
3. Then throw your hands through the ball.

It is as simple as that! The easiest drill for all junior and senior coaches is to have throw-downs (basically a coach throwing balls at the batsman from short range) to improve synch for batsmen. In this case, I recommend throwing the ball under-arm, in a loopy fashion, to make the batsman make every endeavour to get to the pitch of the ball and then provide the power needed for the drive. The harder you throw balls the easier it is for batsmen to hit them. The slower the delivery, the more the batsman has to make sure he does everything right to execute the shot properly.

NERVE TEST

DEAN JONES

It is okay to be nervous. I was always a very nervous starter with the bat, and I had so many inconsistent starts when I was a young player that my father sat me down and asked why. One of his questions was about diet. What did I eat before I went out to bat?

I said: 'Dad, I had cereal, toast with jam, and a cup of tea for breakfast. Then when I got to the ground I had another cup of tea, trained, then some cordial and chewing gum.'

The common factor is that all these foods contain sugar, which is what I gleaned from our little discussion that day. After that, I tried to eliminate sugar from my diet immediately before going out to bat, even to the extent of buying some sugar-free gum. I believe that it helps.

Then I realised that I needed some routines to help me, and before going out to bat, I would place my bat and gloves in a certain way. I remembered that David Boon, my long-time teammate in the Australian team, would always place two chewing gums on top of the peak of his helmet before he sat down waiting his turn to bat.

So when a wicket fell and it was my time to bat, I would stride out to the middle as quick as I could. I would take guard and go through my routine of going down the pitch to do some gardening and allow my eyes to get used to the light. I would stretch a certain way and adjust my padding to get myself comfortable. I noticed later that Ricky Ponting copied it a fair bit and, actually, he used it a lot more effectively than I did.

Between each delivery faced I would look at the ball and the seam when the ball was being thrown back to the bowler. Then I would mark my guard, tap twice with the bat, slot my right foot then left foot into place, and then I looked up to concentrate on the bowler's grip ... and the ball of course. Every good batsman has a routine. Watch them, study them, and find out a routine that works for you and that you can repeat time and time again.

Many batsmen struggle with nerves, and interestingly, we forget to breathe properly when we are anxious. Remember to breathe and when you hit your first few runs, sprint them out as hard as you can to shake off those unwanted nerves. It is great to have nerves; it means that you want to do well. It is a skill, however, to learn to cope with them and shake them off.

SACHIN TENDULKAR

Nerves are a major issue for all players in cricket, but it is about how you manage the butterflies that jump around in your belly. For Sachin Tendulkar, one of the greatest of all batsmen, there were a few tricks to this, and I asked him how he did it. If you watched him closely, it was about habits and routines.

'Every player has nerves,' he told me. 'I certainly had them, but it is how you deal with them that is the trick. It's good to be nervous as you want to do well. I had to deal with my nerves particularly when I played at home in front of packed stadiums and I always felt embarrassed with the adulation the Indian fans showed towards me, but I had to deal with it in some way or another.

'The key I learned was to take my time. To feel comfortable from within, I never wanted to be rushed, so sometimes I might stop to retie my shoe lace at the crease, even though it was perfectly tied already. I would strap and re-strap my pads just to feel comfortable and to get my heart rate down.

'Then I stuck to my routine. I would play the ball, then move three paces towards square leg and then walk the three paces back to my stance. The key for me was to move and never feel static. Everyone is different with their routines. I found my routine and it helped me enormously, so what is yours?'

RAHUL DRAVID

Rahul Dravid of India was known as The Wall, so hard was he to dismiss. A wonderful player, a scorer of 36 Test centuries for India, he offered some advice on finding a way to relax while you are batting — never easy at international level!

'I was such an intense person in my early years as a cricketer,' he told me. 'It worried me, as it reflected in some of my early performances and I needed to find a solution, I needed to find a way to relax. I tended to hang around my room, having room-service meals, and I needed to get out with my teammates to relax. 'Meditation was another method that I found which helped me enormously. It removed a lot of the tension from my body and mind. I also started to read, which was something I had not done much of as a kid. But as I grew older, I started to read more, and now I love it. I read a lot of different fiction and non-fiction books, and it is a great habit to get into.'

For Rahul, it was about clearing a path for himself to walk through. 'I found a couple of diversions to stop me thinking about my game and I found I wasn't "getting in the way of myself". So finding a new diversion from the game could help improve your cricket. Why not go look at the city you are in? Go to the gym or hire a bike for a ride. Find something that interests you, and you will find more solace in your game.'

DONALD BRADMAN

BOUNCED OUT

Playing great fast bowling is a mystery to a lot of batsmen, even good ones.

I grew up in Test cricket facing the most fearsome group of four quicks from the West Indies, right from my first match for Australia, and it was tricky, to say the least.

Once, I asked Sir Donald Bradman how he would play against the West Indies in their pomp, and he said that he would take strike a few centimetres outside leg stump. His reasoning was that with a look at the three stumps, the bowlers would be lured into pitching up more, which is what you wanted as a batsman.

So long as you know where your off stick is, it's irrelevant where you start your stance.

GOING BIG

Have you noticed the batting grips on the biggest power-hitter, or 'bangers', as I call them? Players like Chris Gayle, Andre Russell, Carlos Brathwaite, and Adam Gilchrist all hold the bat very high in the handle. Actually, their handles are made some five centimetres (or two inches) longer than the standard, and they will have three or four grips on them.

The reason for the extra-long handle is that they are very tall men with large hands and massive arms. Holding the bat higher helps them to use the bat and its technologies in the right way. Like a shaft in a golf club, the handle is the most important part of a cricket bat. By holding the bat further up the handle, it allows the handle to be used in the way it's designed to be, creating flex, lag, and power. This maximises their chances of hitting the ball farther.

As we speak today, bat manufacturers are working on different designs to suit players who play Test and T20 cricket. Just when you think enough is enough with the size of the bats, handles will be the next big thing, mark my words.

DON'T PLAY THE MAN: RAHUL DRAVID

Rahul Dravid, the great Indian top-order batsman, was no different from anyone else in that he had certain bowlers who were a problem to him. This is very common; a certain bowler has found a way of getting you out, and it needs to be addressed.

I asked him how he handled this situation.

He said: 'As a kid I watched in awe of the great West Indian fast bowlers like Curtly Ambrose, Courtney Walsh, and Pakistani great Wasim Akram. I dreamed of facing them many times. But this actually was to my detriment, because when the moment arrived and I had my chance to face these greats, I felt that I played the bowler instead of the ball.

'Similarly, when Sri Lanka's Muttiah Muralidaran came along and he had the magical powers of disguising his off spinner and the 'doosra', I had no clue at times as to which way the ball was spinning. What I found was that I needed to prepare myself properly for every single delivery, to stay in the moment, watch the ball, watch the rotation of the ball, and look for the length of the ball.

'I needed to keep it simple and take the face and brand name away from the delivery. I then concentrated on taking two big breaths before each delivery, which was the cue that brought me back into my own space and kept me centred. Preparation before each ball is important. Take one ball at a time, stay in the moment, play straight, and don't look too far ahead.'

RAHUL DRAVID

BALANCE AND INNER DEMONS: RAHUL DRAVID

All batsmen, even the greats, have technical problems at times. Rahul Dravid, the great Indian batsman, found that in his case, it was in his head that the problem lay.

'One of my biggest problems with my technique — and I fought with this for years — was that I had a tendency for my head to fall over towards cover, which would ruin my bat plane and open me up to be dismissed LBW,' he told me.

'I found through meditation that this bad habit wasn't really a technical problem at all, it was mental. I worked out if I felt relaxed, then my balance would come back. The more intense I got, the more unbalanced I became.

'Once I felt relaxed, I went at the ball or, in other words, my head went towards the ball and I wasn't hanging back. In 2008, we were playing England in Mohali and I was facing Stuart Broad. I was so worried because I had only scored one century in the previous two years, and my career was on the line. I needed a hundred badly, and it was my 131st Test and I was a bunch of nerves.

'I played this poor pull shot that went up in the air, and both fieldsmen looked at each other to catch the ball and the ball luckily landed straight in the middle of the two. They both could have caught it in their pocket. At that moment, for some reason, my nerves went, as I gave myself a good talking to. "Stop this rubbish thinking and let's be positive. Let's get after them and get my head to the ball." I went on to make a 136, and it gave me another couple of years playing Test cricket.'

Rahul believes the difference between good and great players is mainly mental capacity. 'I believe the game is about 70 per cent mental, and that sorts the good ones from the bad. Dealing with your negative thoughts and your inner demons is a skill. Only you know what's going on in your head. Your brain can only have one thought at a time, and you just have to find a way to flush out the bad thoughts and bring in the positive thoughts. Once you know how to do that, runs will come your way more consistently.'

WHEN YOU GET OUT

Nowadays, when I play the odd 'friendly' cricket match, I hate it when I get out, maybe even more than when I was playing at the top level. Frankly, it is amazing the thoughts that go through a batsman's head when he has been dismissed. I see players smash their kit up, swear, curse, and holler.

But with hindsight, I think this time is really valuable in the sense that your subconscious is telling you what you did wrong on the field. I think it is important to note things down at the end of the day and remember where you erred. Was it a technique flaw, a strategy flaw, or your gut instinct (blood rush) that caused your demise? This is a time to be honest, very honest, in your assess-ment of your fall of wicket.

I remember at times being happy with a 30-odd that I made, yet furious with myself for getting out at 150! I believe that eight out of ten times you get yourself out through some stupid way or another. So the time afterwards is so important for your development as a batsman because the idea is to make sure it does not happen again.

There are some non-negotiables when batting. I remember getting out to a guy who could not bowl at all. I was so furious with myself that, if a guy came on to bowl who could not bowl, like a David Boon or Mark Taylor, I made sure I milked them and NEVER lifted the ball off the ground so that I made absolutely sure that it did not happen again.

It is bad enough getting out to guys like Malcolm Marshall, Joel Garner, Michael Holding, Curtly Ambrose, Wasim Akram, Waqar Younis, and others. You NEVER get out to bowlers like Boon or Taylor. NEVER!

SPOONER

WHEN A BOWLER OWNS YOU

I had a huge problem when I faced Richard Hadlee, the great New Zealand fast bowler. He was a brilliant bowler as it was, but I was effectively out before I even faced him because, for some reason, I could not read his length, I did not get forward or back, I seemed to have what we call 'diver's boots on' — those heavy boots that deep-sea divers use.

It was the summer of 1985–86, and my father, Barney, sat me down to ask a few pertinent questions. 'Hadlee is all over you. He has got you out four times already, and you are his "bunny". What are we going to do? So what are his strengths?'

I told Dad that Hadlee's length was impeccable and that he could bowl a ball into a shoebox with his eyes shut. Dad said: 'What's his weakness?' I said: 'Doesn't have one!' So Dad said: 'Yes he does. Come and tell me when you've worked it out.'

I never slept a wink that night, but it hit me in the morning. I went to Dad: 'He's predictable. I'm going to bat one metre out of my crease and hit him off his length!'

From then on, Sir Richard never worried me too much, and I made two big ODI hundreds against him on his home soil. He was a champion, Hadlee, and he taught me a lot. At the time, I did not like him, but later I really appreciated what a great player he was, and I am very happy to call him a close friend now.

The point is, if a bowler worries you, find out what his strength is and what his weakness is. Be proactive in hurting him on his weaknesses and make sure your defence is solid and sound when he is attacking you. Be wary when he is on, and be wary when he is tired and hurt him badly.

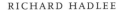

RICHARD HADLEE

YOUR BAT: RICKY PONTING

Ricky Ponting, the former Australian skipper, told me that he was always concerned about bat handles, their degree of flex, and their thickness. 'Some were tighter than others, and I would loosen then up on a hand rail, pushing the handle against it. Other handles were too slim, and I would put tape under the grip to thicken them up.

'I used bats weighing about 2lb 8oz–10oz. I was quite picky with my bats, and even had the handle cut shorter by two centimetres. All the great players wanted to have control of the face of the bat and gripped the bat a little lower than most, which cut down on the huge backlifts that tended to get players into trouble. Mind you, that did not seem to bother Sir Garfield Sobers or Brian Lara, who both had high backlifts!'

MAKE A LIST

Ricky Ponting was an absolute champion No. 3 bat for Australia, and he had a routine that he followed the night before he batted in a match. It involved writing a checklist, which he told me went like this:

1. Watch the ball
2. Play straight
3. Loud calls
4. Be patient
5. Be positive in attack and defence
6. Bat for a long time
7. Make 100
8. Be Man of the Match
9. Be the Man of the Series
10. How are the bowlers going to get me out?
11. Visualise how they will try to get me out
12. Then sleep!

I do like that kind of thinking, and that level of planning. It is worth a try, for sure.

RUNNING BETWEEN THE WICKETS

It is very easy to be a good runner between the wickets. In the Australian team, it was a focus but in some teams, it is one of those things that slips through the cracks. My keys are these:

1. Run on the pitch and run in straight lines.
2. When running a lot of twos, make sure you take enough time to get your heart rate

back to an appropriate level when you face the next ball. I always took a while to walk back to my crease if I was running a lot of ones and twos. You control the tempo of the match, not them.

3. When backing up at the bowler's end, stay side-on, not front-on. This makes it easier to stop and turn back to the bowler's end when under pressure.

4. The key to fast running between the wickets is to time your turn. I used the bowler's danger area to place my left foot down, then put my left hand down and slide my bat past the crease by two centimetres. Work out what is a 'comfortable turning circle' for you and make a mark on the side of the pitch.

5. RUN AND TURN IN STRAIGHT LINES! IT IS NOT HARD.

6. Between overs, always discuss with your partner where there is an easy single to be had, and which fieldsman might have a weakness — someone that you can steal a run from.

GRIP PRESSURE: KEVIN PIETERSEN

One issue that is not often talked about in analysis of batting is grip pressure. I think it is extremely important, and I went to Kevin Pietersen, the brilliant England batsman, for some thoughts on this. Not surprisingly, he also considers it important. Pietersen told me he changed his grip pressure constantly against different bowlers and depending where he wanted to hit the ball.

'If I was facing a spinner and there were opportunities of hitting through the off side, then I would really concentrate on having a very loose grip,' he told me. 'When I was looking to score heavily on the leg side I would tighten my grip and close the face of my bat before the bowler released the ball. The key to this is not to play across the line of the ball, just let the angle of the bat face allow the ball to go through the leg side. A lot of batsmen manipulate the face of their bats to where they would like to hit the ball.

'Grip pressure is such a personal thing. For example, in golf the great golfer Arnold Palmer would grip the club quite tightly, and yet other greats like Jack Nicklaus and Greg Norman would be the opposite. It is just trial and error. Just make sure your bottom hand doesn't overtake your top hand.

'The top hand of your grip is the power hand, and the lower hand is the steering wheel. If your bottom hand has a tendency of taking over, then try what Adam Gilchrist tried in the 2007 World Cup final — taping a half a squash ball to his lower hand to allow his top hand to dominate his bat plane. That allowed him to hit through the line and through the ball better. If you can't find a squash ball, try a stone or coin. It gives the same result.

REVERSE SWEEPING: KEVIN PIETERSEN

The reverse sweep was hardly even around when I played, but of course it is commonplace now. And one of the first to master it, and to take the shot on when it was considered by conservatives to be a no-no, was Kevin Pietersen of England. Pietersen equated it with a backhand shot in squash, of which he was a fan.

I asked him for some keys for this shot, which is so valuable against stacked leg-side fields. He told me: 'Before you even try to play the reverse sweep, make sure you have got the technique and sequence by practising it properly in the nets. Secondly, when you do think about playing it, make sure you have made a score in the previous match!

'Believe me when I say this, if you get out to a reverse sweep, the selectors and the media sharpen their red pens. Just ask Mike Gatting (whose infamous reverse sweep dismissal possibly cost England the 1987 World Cup final) and lately Glenn Maxwell when they get out to these shots!

'Bowlers hate being reverse swept and I loved doing it because they go bananas if you pull it off. Firstly, quickly change your grip to a left-hand batsman's grip and make sure the bat face is looking towards the covers or point. The actual "motion" of the shot is no different to playing a back-handed shot like you do in squash or tennis. I was very good at squash and I felt playing the reverse sweep was just as easy as it is playing the conventional sweep shot.

'The key here, like any other shot, is to really watch the ball onto the bat. I see a lot of kids and seniors take a little peek at where they want the ball to go instead of really watching the ball onto the bat. And PLEASE wear a helmet when attempting this shot.'

KEVIN PIETERSEN

THE SWITCH HIT:
KEVIN PIETERSEN

The switch hit has caused controversy, with some people saying that it should be declared illegal. It involves switching from left-handed to right-handed as the bowler delivers, and playing the shot. David Warner is one famous example of someone who has pulled it off, and while the rule-makers have left it in place, the fact is it is a very difficult shot to play.

I asked Kevin Pietersen of England, one who has managed it a few times, to explain the keys. He told me that a player needed to get his sequence exactly right, and that it could only work against certain players.

He told me the sequence is:

1. Move your hands into a left-hand batsman's grip. For me, the left hand is lower than the right hand on the grip.

2. Make sure the bat face is pointing to where you want to hit the ball.
3. Now quickly jump or move to a left-hander's stance, with your backside pointing towards point.
4. Don't over hit it, watch the ball onto the bat and let it fly.

Kevin said he preferred to play it against spinners, mainly leg spinners. 'The reason why leg spinners is my first choice is that they generally do not have time to change their delivery if I happen to go into the shot "too early". Interestingly, I learned to play these shots at the age of 25, so if you study the movements and sequences, and practise properly to get the confidence to execute the shot, it should be a breeze when playing in a match.'

THE NERVOUS 90s

A lot of batsmen at all levels get nervous when they reach the 90s, although I must admit I never ever really worried about it. Put simply, batsmen must realise that there is nothing too ugly about getting out in the 90s. In fact, if any person walked up to me and gave me 90-odd I would take it any day of the week.

Yes, it's true that we do focus on batsmen who make many hundreds. But my method was to not be concerned about the three or four I might need to post a century; I was thinking about how many runs I would make *after* 100.

I did have one problem when I was 98 not out with one over to go when we played a Test match in Perth against Sri Lanka. I said to myself that I will not be going to bed tonight sleeping on 98, and I wanted my hundred in the last over of the day. Sure enough, on the fifth ball of that last over I took a big leg-side swipe at an Aravinda de Silva delivery and I was dropped at mid-wicket, lucky to scramble the two I needed.

I was so embarrassed with the shot that I could not raise my bat and accept the applause from the crowd, nor my teammates in the dressing room, the group of them having come out onto the balcony to acknowledge me. What I noticed was that Allan Border, our captain, was not among them.

Soon enough I found out why. When I walked off the ground, I could not bear to go into the rooms and cop a gob full of abuse from the infamous 'Captain Grumpy', Border, so I walked straight up into the viewing room and waited for 40 minutes for the dressing room to clear. However 'AB' was waiting and he did not miss me, lecturing me about what my duty of care should have been for the team and our score. Ultimately, I was out first ball the next day, but it was a lesson for me.

When you get nervous in the 90s, go through your routines and just remember how you made your 90-plus runs in the first place. Don't change anything; trust that your natural game will get the runs without being too impatient. Enjoy the journey of your innings and just remember it is better to be out in the middle batting than sitting on your backside!

BATTING AGAINST REVERSE SWING

I was so lucky to play against the greatest exponents of reverse-swing bowling, the likes of Imran Khan, Wasim Akram, and Waqar Younis of Pakistan. It was bad enough anytime facing these guys, as they bowled like lightning, but not only could they swing the new ball, they seemed even deadlier when the ball was 40 overs old.

Let's take Wasim Akram, for example. Not only was he the greatest left-arm bowler of all time, 'Waz' could bowl the most lethal reverse-swinging deliveries ever. Just look at the high-lights tape of the 1992 World Cup final and it will tell you exactly how good he was.

These great fast bowlers tried to set you up with a series of bouncers, then they would try in-swinging fast yorkers to knock your toes off your feet. It was quite a bizarre time to play cricket in the 1980s and 1990s as the West Indian fast bowlers tried to kill you with fast bouncers, while the Pakistani quicks tried to break your toes with reverse-swing bowling.

The big trick for the Pakistani bowlers was to work on one side of the ball. They never put spit onto the ball, just polished it as much as they could, with the other side of the ball getting really roughed up. Their fieldsmen would often return the ball short of the keeper or bowler, so they would scuff up one side of the ball, and there was a technique where they would keep the seam horizontal, like the rings of Saturn, to scuff the ball up.

The other neat little trick was that the Pakistani bowlers would run in with both hands covering up the ball and their grip, so that the batsman could not tell which way the bowler was trying to swing it.

SO HERE IS THE SECRET: Always look for length first and foremost. These guys are bowling two lengths, one at your head, the other at your toes.

1. The Kookaburra ball used in Australia had two distinctive colours to it when it was properly 'prepared' by the Pakistani bowlers. The shiny side would look dark, and the scuffed-up or rough side looked lighter in colour. All I did was to look for the dark, shiny side. When Wasim Akram had the shiny or dark side facing the leg side, it would be an in-swinger; when the shiny side faced the off side, it would be an away-swinger.

2. When facing reverse-swing bowling, the ball will always swing late compared to new-ball bowling or conventional swing. So the key to facing reverse-swing bowling is to PLAY THE BALL LATE. The ball must be played under your nose, not out in front of you. If you go hard at the ball when it's reverse swinging, you will be back in the dressing rooms before you know it!

3. Bat on a leg-stump guard. Sit very side-on to the delivery. And, what I say will shock you, but do not try to use your feet, let the ball come to you and just try and deflect the ball. Their swing is your strength: allow their swing to create holes in the field, just deflecting it away.

PLAYING SPIN: SOURAV GANGULY

Indians generally play spin well, I guess because they grow up on turning pitches on the subcontinent, and Sourav Ganguly was one of the best, in my view. Ganguly played 113 Tests and 311 one-day internationals for India, and captained with distinction as well. I asked Sourav for some ideas about playing against high-quality spin, and interestingly, he felt that against the best, a batsman needed to be aggressive.

'I played on big turning pitches, so firstly, your forward and back defensive shots better be rock solid first,' he said. 'Once that part of your game is in order, then work out how you will score. When I played against a spinner, I never wanted him to settle. Never ever! I would bat on different guards and would get way forward or deep into my crease on the back foot.

'When I played against the greats like Shane Warne and Muttiah Muralidaran, I would always be looking to go after them. These guys never bowled bad balls, so you had to go after them, to force them to make a mistake. I always wanted to show my intent, just enjoy the battle. Show good body language when going after quality spinners, or any bowler for that matter.

SOURAV GANGULY

'Just think you have a great defence to keep their good balls out, and know where you can hit them for four and where you can get a single to get off strike.'

TRYING TO HIT A BIG ONE

Everyone thinks that the big bats are the reason why the batsmen of today are hitting it big, and they certainly are one factor, but not the main reason, in my opinion. The batsmen of today are allowed to work on their techniques of trying to hit it big in the nets, they do more weights, and no doubt the boundaries are shorter.

The key to hitting it big is to use your core and how quickly you can rotate your hips. Just look at the big power-hitters of today, the likes of Chris Gayle, David Warner, Kevin Pietersen, Andre Russell, Virat Kohli, MS Dhoni, and AB de Villiers. They all get deep into their crease, load up into the back leg like a baseball pitcher or a golfer, then press forward and rotate their core and hips as quickly as they can.

This creates lag in the arms and bat, and creates huge amounts of torque and kinetic rotating energy, which results in faster bat and hand speed. When you watch the slow-motion replays of these guys when they hit a massive six, when they get the bat to the top of their back swing, the first movement is their lower half or core, and everything else follows after that.

So to practise this, get 20 old balls, go to the middle of the oval, and ask someone to throw you waist-height balls and try to hit the ball for six by rotating your core and hips fast and furious first and foremost on the downswing. When you start to see the ball disappear over the fence, don't forget to thank me! You're welcome.

VVS LAXMAN

BATTING ... AND BATTING: VVS LAXMAN

VVS Laxman was a beautiful player, elegant and effective, too, a man who played at his best against the better teams. Against Australia, for instance, he was absolutely brilliant, including his famous 281 against the rampant Aussies at Eden Gardens in Kolkata in 2001, inspiring one of the greatest of all Test comebacks.

No wonder they nicknamed him 'Very, Very Special'! He batted with Rahul Dravid through an entire day in that particular match, and I wanted to talk to him about batting for long periods — what the secrets were.

'My uncle once told me at a very young age, "Just bat session by session." This piece of advice stopped me from getting ahead of myself, and *made sure* that I played the MERIT of the ball. I loved batting at No. 3 for India, where I had certain types of disciplines.

'I always thought the first hour I batted was owned by the bowler. The first hour was all about getting used to the bounce and pace of the pitch. The second hour, however, was a time for me to open up, a bit like a flower about to blossom, so to speak.

'Like Deano's father, who said to him, "Just bat time," my mantra was to break the day up, and bat session by session, and this helped me relax and just play the ball on its own merits. Doing this, I found the day to go very quickly indeed.'

TIMING AND ACCURACY: VVS LAXMAN

Virtually nobody timed the ball like VVS Laxman. He is one of the most beautiful players that I have ever had the privilege to watch, with those wristy flicks and gorgeous drives. But every batsman, including one with the talent of Laxman, has problems with piercing the field.

It is a big problem for some players, and it has to be addressed. I asked VVS for some thoughts.

'Deano mentioned earlier in the book that if he continued to hit the ball to the field, he would change guard or bat outside his crease. If the pitch was spinning square, sometimes I would bat on off stump, particularly to an off spinner who might be turning the ball.

'But the one thing I concentrated on, mostly, was thinking about my impact position when hitting the ball. I concentrated on hitting or meeting the ball earlier, or I would try to hit the ball much later. This, funnily enough, improved my timing at times, and no doubt improved my scoring opportunities.

'So when you are in the nets, either by facing some bowlers or through throwdowns, try to hit the ball earlier, and the next ball, try to hit the ball much later. You will find by hitting the ball earlier, the ball will go straighter, and by hitting the ball later, the ball will go a lot squarer. These subtleties, my friends, are the very key elements of what makes a good batsman!'

TEND YOUR PITCH: VVS LAXMAN

Batting is a craft, and there are subtleties to it. Such as keeping the workplace clean, so to speak. I talked to India's great VVS Laxman about this, and he is red hot on it.

'I always tried to keep the pitch clean of any debris when I batted,' he told me. 'It's my office, so I tried to keep it as neat as I could. Proper maintenance of a pitch and the bowlers' footholds is imperative to making consistently big scores. When I saw holes in the pitch, I tried to fill them up with some of the small bits of pitch and smashed it in with my bat.

'I know in Australia, they tried to keep the holes free of any debris, but I feel this style of pitch preparation is the wrong way. The Australians tend to kick off any small bits of turf and not fill in these holes that sometimes leave sharp edges to them. These sharp edges can make the ball kick and take off at awkward angles.

'In India, depending on certain types of pitches, we try to fill in these holes on the pitch with any debris that might be on the pitch. When the ball lands on the repaired area, we find that the ball will not react as severely.

'So I recommend that a batsman cleans his house properly, and makes it a part of his routine. Even being disciplined about how you walk around the danger areas, making sure you are keeping your pitch clean and intact, is a discipline all batsmen need to follow. Stay off the danger areas with your spikes, even when you go to speak to your batting partner. It's amazing how many players walk right down the pitch, causing it to deteriorate even further!'

THE SLOWER BALL

BOWLING TIPS

FOOT FAULTS: WASIM AKRAM

I talked to Wasim Akram about boots, and how important they are for a bowler, especially a quick bowler. It cannot be understated. When a fast bowler lands his or her front foot in the delivery stride, the front foot will carry 15 times their body weight through it, all reverberating through the foot, the ankle, the knee, and the hip.

Needless to say, you need the right footwear to take account of that fact. Wasim, the great Pakistani left-armer, told me: 'Some bowlers, like Imran Khan, Waqar Younis, Dennis Lillee, Jeff Thomson, Rodney Hogg, and others wore a heavy leather-soled boot, but I hated these style of boots, as I was quite light on my feet. I bowled in what we call half-spikes.

'I carried three pairs of boots with me, but some bowlers would carry up to six pairs, slowly breaking them in at practice before using them in matches. But the major secret for me was that I wore three very thick socks on each foot. Socks are the key, and buy the best ones you can find.

'Nowadays, a lot of bowlers *cut* a little hole in the boot over the big toe of the foot that lands in front in the delivery stride — in my case, the right toe.

It alleviated a lot of pressure from my toe, and I did not lose too many toenails! Even though I did not strap my ankles, I think many bowlers should, particularly at practice.'

WASIM AKRAM

TIP: TEMPO IS EVERYTHING

I have faced guys with huge run-ups like Michael Holding and short run-ups like Wasim Akram. Both were very fast, but both were doing

what we call 'hitting the crease' with power and tempo.

I see so many bowlers start their run-up at top pace and when they hit the crease or get into their delivery action, they are actually reducing pace. This leads to what I call a 'decel', or deceleration, in their actions and arm speeds.

I remember in conversation with the great Richie Benaud, that he could not understand why more bowlers didn't bowl like Jeff Thomson, one of the fastest bowlers ever for Australia in the 1970s and 1980s, and a slinger who bowled off a shortish run-up. Richie thought his action was outstanding, and similar to greats like Fred Spofforth, one of Australia's all-time greats from the 19th century, and a little like Mitchell Johnson's slingshot action.

What these bowlers do more is that they use their core and hips more to get a faster arm speed. It is similar to a golfer, a discus thrower, and other power sports when acceleration is required immediately, so when you are trying to bowl fast, concentrate more on your use of your core and hips and less on your arm and grip. Trust me, the ball will come out quicker.

CONVENTIONAL SWING: THE AKRAM WAY

Wasim Akram was the king of swing bowling in my era, a champion for Pakistan and a vital member of that team's famous World Cup win in 1992. He believes that swinging the ball is as important as it ever was, especially with pitches often being flat and benign.

He told me: 'Why bowlers try to bounce guys out in the first session of a day 1 in a Test match is bewildering to me. Sure, use the odd one short, but the opening bowlers must try to swing the ball by keeping it up.

'I was so lucky to have a great leader and captain like Imran Khan,

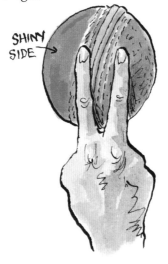

SHINY SIDE

CONVENTIONAL SWING
(BALL SWINGS IN THE DIRECTION
THE SEAM IS POINTING)

because he knew the importance of trying to swing it early. Sure, I will be driven a few times by batsmen happy to get on the front foot, but I will get more batsmen out by pitching up than bowling back of a length.

'The key to swinging the ball is to keep a light grip and secondly the flick of the wrist with the fingers going down the ball ... not across it. This is the major point. The bowler has to keep the energy behind the ball by flicking their fingers to six o'clock on the dial, rather than to five o'clock or seven o'clock.

'The grip is also important. The fingers can be together or apart, but I preferred them to be together. Others like the great Ray Lindwall, Australia's fast bowler of years gone by, would have his fingers placed on both sides of the seam. It's a personal preference only.

'I always loved the saying: "If he misses, I will hit his stumps." It is simple but it is accurate, and 52 per cent of my dismissals in Test and one-day cricket were bowled or LBW.'

THE YORKER: WASIM AKRAM

There is no doubt the yorker, the ball that jams the batsman up, remains in vogue, especially in the shorter forms of the game. But it is also lethal in Test match cricket, and there was no one who did it better than Wasim Akram, Pakistan's magnificent left-armer.

I asked Wasim what the key was. 'I loved bowling yorkers,' he said. 'There was nothing better than hitting a batsman on the boot with a swinging yorker, and this delivery is a great weapon to use against batsmen who have balance problems or have a tendency to allow their head to fall across towards cover.

'To bowl this type of delivery properly, I had to use every bit of energy I could muster. The ball had to be delivered with a quick arm, it had to be very accurate, giving the batsmen no width, and it took a lot out of me.

'The key to success when bowling the yorker was to have your eyes level at ball-release, and to concentrate halfway up the off stump. I would usually aim just below the manufacturer's or sponsor's logo on the middle or off stump, and I practised a lot bowling the yorker from over and around the wicket. Actually, I would spend 30 per cent of my time bowling around the wicket at practice.

'Today's best exponent of the yorker would probably be Sri Lanka's fast bowler in Lasith Malinga. He would practise for hours in the nets by placing a pair of old cricket boots where the batsmen stood. Basically, if you cannot bowl the yorker well, then ODI and T20 cricket will sort you out in a hurry, as it's your last line of defence for a bowler.'

REVERSE SWING: WASIM AKRAM

It was Imran Khan, Pakistan's former captain, who taught Wasim Akram how to bowl reverse swing, the ball that swings the opposite way to conventional swing. Akram became one of the best

exponents of reverse swing, which quickly became a huge factor for bowlers all around international cricket.

Wasim Akram regarded Imran as not only a great captain but a great coach, and Imran passed on the method to his protégés. This is how Wasim describes the way to bowl good reverse swing.

1. Pick up an old ball from the practice bag. Really work hard on one side to get a shine. Keep the other side scuffed up. Sure, you can rough it up on *one* side even more to help you get the understandings of how to bowl reverse swing.

2. The key is to have a very vertical wrist, but your hand and fingers must be pointing to either third man or fine leg. Here is the key: if I was bowling a reverse away-swinger to Deano, I would try to release and spin behind the ball to keep the seam spinning level, as if the seam looked like it was coming at him like ten to four on a clock dial. To swing the ball back into a right-hand batsman like Deano, I would release the ball with my hand and fingers in a more vertical position, with the seam coming at Deano more like 12.30 on the clock dial.

3. I always thought the ball reversed more when I bowled into the breeze, and if you have a cross breeze, then even better. Your fields should not be too attacking, just the one slip with a bat-pad fieldsman as well, maybe two fieldsmen back for the hook as I am bowling two different lengths to upset the batsman's thoughts and process. Make sure you practise to keep the seam level when it's delivered, as a scrambled seam will not reverse swing. The trick is in its release.

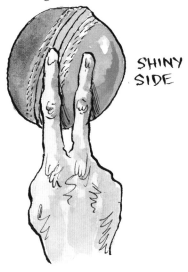

SHINY SIDE

REVERSE SWING
(BALL SWINGS IN THE DIRECTION
THE SEAM IS POINTING)

TEMPO: WAQAR YOUNIS

Waqar Younis was a wonderful fast bowler for Pakistan over a long period of time, and he has been successful beyond his playing career as a coach and commentator. One of the keys to his success was rhythm and tempo, which I took up with him. It is a point worth noting for a young fast bowler who has had problems with no-balls, for instance.

'I had massive problems with my run up and tempo, and the great Imran Khan helped me to get it all sorted,' Waqar told me. 'On the side of the oval, Imran would ask me to run and bowl and not be worried about where the crease or landing areas were to deliver the ball. Slowly I found a rhythm and a run-up distance that I was happy with, and I felt I was accelerating through the crease.

'It took six months to properly sort out the length of my run-up, and that ended up being 32 paces as I marked it out. We also worked out that I needed a marker somewhere through my run-up to maintain tempo and confidence that everything was right. That marker was put down at 16 paces, so I had two markers to help me get my run-up right. I hit those markers with my right foot.

'I never looked at the crease when delivering the ball to see if my feet were in the right position, and I feel this is a huge no-no for young bowlers. How can you look at the crease, to see if your feet are behind the front line, and then concentrate on what spot you are trying to deliver the ball to?

'The big key or image I had in my delivery stride was that I gather my body into a slingshot position. My bottom half was the handle of the slingshot, and my top half was supple and turning and ready to fire.'

WAQAR YOUNIS

SPOONER

NATHAN LYON

MORE SPIN

Nathan Lyon has become Australia's most successful Test off spinner after originally working as a groundsman. I asked him what were the keys at a moment when he was trying to extract more spin. He said that the key was arm speed.

'It's about arm speed and the rotation of your body at release,' he told me. 'The trick for me is to "spin up on the back of the ball". This action creates more overspin, dip, and bounce, which all spinners crave.

'The key to your arm speed is no different to casting a lure from a fishing rod. Now, imagine your arm is a fishing rod, the tip of your rod being your wrist, hand, and fingers. To get maximum spin or revolutions of the ball, my wrist, hands, and fingers must be supple. The spinning finger I used was my right index finger, and I imagined it to spin up on the back of the ball, creating maximum turn for me.

'Interestingly, great off spinners like (Sri Lanka's) Muttiah Muralidaran and (Australia's) Bruce Yardley used their middle finger to spin the ball. Their reason was that the middle finger is the longest on their hand, thus providing the biggest lever. Physicists and biomechanists would always say the biggest levers create the most kinetic energy, so if you want to bowl off spin with a lot of revolutions, try using the right

index as the power finger to spin the ball or your middle finger.

'But please, remember to "Spin up"!'

EMBRACE AGGRESSION

Good batsmen will get after a spinner, and right there is a challenge for the bowler. Does he go into his shell, or does he welcome it? Nathan Lyon, Australia's highly successful off spinner, told me that he was happy to see a batsman attack him.

'This is a time not to panic,' he said. 'Being a top-line spinner means that you better have lots of courage. Yes, you will be hit for six, plenty of times. Being under pressure from a batsman who is trying to hit you to another orbit is what being a spin bowler is all about.'

Lyon said he enjoyed the challenge and preferred an aggressive opponent to a 'stone-waller'. He offered up a few thoughts for spin bowlers who find themselves under the blowtorch:

1. Change your pace and don't be predictable. Remember, if he misses, you hit his stumps. This is a good time to bowl a slider, or arm ball. Slow yourself down a bit in between balls, and make

sure that you own the tempo of the match, not the batsman.

2. Remember that this is NOT a time to be afraid. Don't be frightened to have what we call 'in-out fields'. This means a slip and bat-pad and a deep mid-on and mid wicket.

3. England's great batsman Kevin Pietersen loved going after me and he hated taking singles. He wanted boundaries, which is why batsmen like him do not like 'in-out fields'.

4. You will be getting messages from your sub-conscious, so just follow your gut instinct on what type of ball you want to bowl, what line and at what pace. Just remember, if you give the batsman pace, it allows him to hit it further.

FOUR KEY WORDS

When Australia's Nathan Lyon is struggling with his off spinners, he has four points that he goes back to. This is important for any bowler, to have a fallback position — some key points to call upon when the batsman is on top.

Lyon told me: 'When I feel I am not bowling well, I try to bowl around the wicket. By doing this, for me to land the ball in the right areas, I have to use my big muscles and rotate properly over my front foot. But there are some times I feel like the ball is as heavy as a bowling ball.

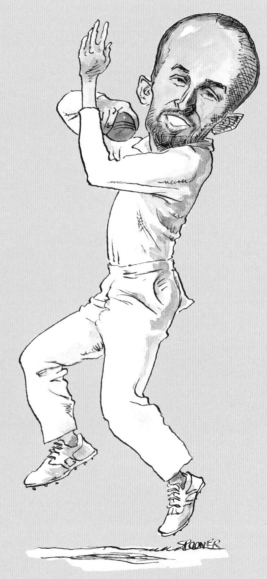

NATHAN LYON

'So here are some buzzwords or keywords for me to get me in the right shape when bowling the ball:

1. UP: meaning get my left arm or front arm as high as I can
2. OVER: rotate my body and allow my bowling arm to go over my front leg
3. COCK: when my back foot lands down in my delivery stride, cock my wrist in a position where I feel I can rip it
4. THROUGH: follow through and maintain momentum when bowling through the crease and towards my target.

'Now when you have found some good rhythm and momentum, own the tempo of the over. Quickly turn and get into the over. Do not allow the batsman to hold you up when you are on top.

'I always worked with my keeper after every over. I asked him: "How was my speed? Were my revs good? What tactics should we try for the next over?" Always communicate with your captain as well, or Captain Grumpy might appear!'

THE BOWLER'S DEFENCE

Like any good batsmen, every good bowler has an offence and a defence. A bowler's offence is speed, swing, and spin. His defence is being able to bowl the ball in the so-called 'corridor of uncertainty', where a batsman does not know when to go forward or back. This length for a quick bowler is four to six metres from the batsman or for a spinner two to four metres away.

Interestingly, the firebrand Australian Shaun Tait bowled one of the quickest deliveries ever at the MCG of 160.7 km/h in a one-day international, and the crowd went ballistic when it was announced on the electronic scoreboards. The thing that made me laugh was that the batsman should have hit it for four as it was right in the slot to drive it down the ground!

Why were Shane Warne, Glenn McGrath, Dennis Lillee, Wasim Akram, and Sir Richard Hadlee great? Yes, they could bowl quickly and spin it miles, but they bowled impeccable lines and lengths when under pressure. You can be super quick like Tait, but batsmen still sorted him out because he lacked a proper line and length when conditions favoured the batsmen.

It is interesting to find out what the right length is for each batsman, as they are all different. For example, for Hadlee to bowl a 'good length' to me it was four to six metres from the batting crease, but if he was trying to bowl the right length to Steve Smith, the current Australian captain, for instance, Hadlee would need to bowl the ball fuller, at around three to five metres from the crease. The reason being that Smith has a premeditated back-and-across movement at point of delivery.

What ruins both a batsman's and a bowler's form first is that their defence lets them down, not their offence.

Bowlers must hit their targets and be repetitive, and hope the fieldsmen take the catches that might be on offer.

AS A KID, BOWL IT FAST, OR RIP IT

Cricket Australia has a huge database on players in my country, keeping tabs on every player from the age of 15. At an early age, scouts or talent-identifying officers will mainly look for kids' offensive skills — for instance, often looking at how fast they are bowling. Mitchell Starc, the left-armer who has done so well in recent times, was identified at 16 when he was bowling around 135 km/h.

We also love to see kids who can really spin the ball, or batsmen who can hit it a long way. Another offensive skill that is sometimes ignored by many is the time a batsman has when playing a ball. Just look at batsmen like Mark Waugh and Damien Martyn, who both seemed to have enough time to knit a jumper when the quicks were bowling to them.

As coaches, we can easily teach defensive skills for bowlers. What we cannot teach a kid is to bowl at 160 km/h or spin it like a Shane Warne, Stuart MacGill, or Nathan Lyon. So I tell all

kids to go out there and try to bowl it as fast as they can or spin it as hard as they can when they are young, especially if they want to be noticed. In other words, work on your offensive skills first as a kid and let the defensive stuff come later.

WICKETKEEPING TIPS

THE 'PERFECT' ROOMMATE

Ian Healy was one of the greatest wicketkeepers of all time, playing for Australia with distinction for more than ten years in one of his country's greatest eras. You never heard a ball go into his gloves because they were so soft and supple.

Even though he looked like Barney Rubble in *The Flintstones*, he was one of the best teammates to have. Heals always had a 'winners' shirt, and it would be so loud and awful and only worn on days that we won. He was loved by one and all.

I roomed with Ian Healy for many years and he was almost the perfect roommate. Almost! Heals would get up every morning at 6.30 am and try not to wake his 'roomy'. He would put his shirt and shorts on and groan in pain when trying to tie his shoelaces up.

Then he would carefully and quietly go to the bathroom, still trying not to wake me up, start singing while he was cleaning his teeth, whilst still thinking I was asleep. It was annoying, I can tell you. I can honestly say that Heals continued to completely butcher Cher's song 'If I Could Turn Back Time'.

Then he would grab his inners and a golf ball, proceeding to grab my big toe, and say, 'Just going down to the basement to catch a few balls, Deano. Hope I didn't wake you?' Really, it was the groaning when doing his shoes up that got me.

But he would come back into the room dripping in a lather of sweat. His dedication to craft and to his teammates was beyond reproach. All I know is that whenever I heard an opposition batsman knick a ball, start walking, pal — Heals never missed them!

WHEN YOU STRUGGLE: IAN HEALY

Ian Healy was, like the best of keepers, largely invisible, because he was so efficient, so good behind the stumps. But it was not always so easy for him, he told me.

'Like batsmen and bowlers, keepers also struggle at times,' he said. 'I would always go with the adage:
- Stop thinking
- Just want the ball ... WITH ENERGY!
- Don't worry about your feet
- Make sure when you take the ball the bowler can see your squatchee on your cap
- Wait for the ball. Take the ball just in front of your body
- Make sure contact of the ball is in your peripheral vision.'

THE GOLF-BALL DRILL: IAN HEALY

Ian Healy's golf-ball drill became a bit of an urban legend in its own right. For more than a decade, Australia's all-time great keeper had a habit of disappearing down to the hotel car park while he was on tour and practising his craft.

I asked him why it was so important, and what it was about.

'I loved my golf-ball drill,' he said. 'Find a metre-high wall, and wear your "inners" for this only. Throw the ball into the wall on the full, and make the ball bounce just before you catch it. This is a great drill to work on your body position, but make sure:
- You keep the weight on the balls of your feet
- Your backside is pointing down
- Your back is straight
- You concentrate on your contact points
- You move quickly left and right
- You COMPLETE THE PROPER SEQUENCE: head to the ball, then feet, then your hands.'

UP TO THE STUMPS: IAN HEALY

Keepers are really defined by how they perform when they are up to the stumps for the slower bowlers. Being a keeper is a crazy-difficult skill to perfect, and it is really a sight to behold when you see a good one. I will never forget how well Ian Healy kept up to the stumps when Shane Warne was bowling, especially on big-turning tracks.

When I asked him for a tip about this, he said that going up to the stumps sorted out most keepers. Heals said: 'Firstly, always wear a helmet. And when keeping to spinners, ALWAYS HAVE YOUR HEAD OVER YOUR GLOVES!

'A good drill for this is to have an old chair with the back and seat taken out of it. Place it where the batsmen would stand and get balls thrown under, around, and through the chair. Sure, there will be deflections, but it makes you watch the ball very closely and is a lot of fun.'

IAN HEALY

CAPTAINCY TIPS

THE THREE Vs: RICKY PONTING

Ricky Ponting captained Australia in 77 Tests, with a brilliant winning record of 64 per cent, as well as skippering the Aussies to World Cup wins in 2003 and 2007. He told me that he was a believer in the so-called three Vs of captaincy. That is: Vision, Values, and Validation.

'What is the team's style of play? That needs to be a *vision*. Let the team believe and take ownership in that style of play. The captain, along with the senior group, must create a set of behaviours of what the teams does together in order to achieve the goals the team has set itself.

'These are the *values*, and this is what we call *culture*, and the squad must adhere to it and believe in it. No doubt if we have the right game style, coupled with the right culture and discipline, the results will look after themselves, which gives you the *validation* of what they believe in.

'Get the team together and find a style of game that you can play. Keep it simple and straightforward, and above all have some fun, and results will look after themselves.'

RICKY PONTING

INSTINCT IS KING: SOURAV GANGULY

Sourav Ganguly was a terrific captain for India, leading his country for five years and 49 Tests, becoming India's most successful overseas captain. He was combative, and he had ideas. I asked him for some of his themes.

'I always wanted to keep ahead of the game,' he told me. 'I had a style of game that I believed in, and always wanted to get control of the game. The whole team must believe in this style of the game as well.

'I was blessed to have captained many greats of Indian cricket, guys like Sachin Tendulkar, Rahul Dravid, Anil Kumble, Virender Sehwag, VVS Laxman, and many more. But I needed to create an environment where they could express their brilliant talents with freedom. I needed them to believe in the style of game I wanted the team to play and let them know exactly what role I wanted them to play.

'Fortunately, I was so lucky that not only were they great players they were great human beings, too. This helps so much and made my job so easy as a captain. Once you have this talent, you next job is to make sure you don't overburden them with too many long and boring team meetings. Then captain with your gut instincts. It's so important to listen to the players' thoughts, but ultimately it is down to you as their captain, and your decision is final.

'I loved being captain, but ultimately it's about knowing exactly what your players can do in the middle. Then strategise around their strengths. So get to know your players. Understand what makes them tick, and then use their strengths to your advantage.'

PROBLEM PLAYERS

There is a great sign at my local golf club. It reads: 'BEFORE YOU COMPLAIN, HAVE YOU VOLUNTEERED YET?'

I love this quote. Many cricket clubs around the world have people who give enormous amounts of free time for the sake of their club and the game of cricket, and that feeling is sometimes ruined by many players within the club complaining about something or other or filling the place with negativity.

The reality is that every team has a player who requires more maintenance than others. Many players can be disruptive or seem to show no care for the team's vision or game plan.

I am currently the coach of the Islamabad United franchise in the Pakistan Super League — not that I have problems with any of my players! But I do have problems with some of them going to sleep in my ten-minute coach's meeting before the game!

When we qualified to play in the semi-final of the PSL in 2016, I asked the West Indian players Andre Russell and Sam Badree to conduct the meeting and come up with notions

of what they thought we should concentrate on to win the match.

Well, Sam Badree had been a school teacher for five or more years, and he gave the squad puzzles to think of to ease the tension. Everyone had some fun and enjoyed the mind battles with Sam.

When Andre came up to speak, we had no idea what he was about to say or do, because he is a typical happy-go-lucky guy, very friendly, always laughing, and so cool. But he spoke about how much winning this match meant to him, about how much fun he had enjoyed with the squad. Andre told us that it was time to believe in ourselves, believe that we could accomplish anything that we wanted, and he spoke with so much passion that everyone was so amped up. It was unbelievable.

We won the semi-final, went on to triumph in the final, and I always look back on that meeting and how it changed the team's focus and belief in how good they were.

So sometimes it might be good to give the responsibility to a difficult or disruptive player and see if they can lead. Let them embarrass themselves or lead you out of the bad-form patch the team might be in. You might be surprised at what you find!

MEDIA MATTERS: MICHAEL CLARKE

Michael Clarke was a highly successful captain of Australia because he regarded it as an honour and a privilege. But he told me that being captain of a high-profile and top-level team carried burdens that were unforeseen.

'One of the hardest jobs is dealing with the constant barrage of the media, from, TV, radio, newspapers, and other media platforms — they are all trying to get an exclusive story in some shape or form.

'No doubt it is at its hardest when the team loses or when a player has been dropped. The media have a way of editing and twisting things to suit their own agendas.'

This rang true to me, and I remember the great Greg Norman once said he preferred to do live interviews as the media network could not edit his words in any way to suit the notions of the reporter.

As Michael points out, though, a captain can use the media platform in a positive way, too: 'It is a perfect place to remind people what the vision is, and the focus the team is working on at the time, and it is also a great time to remind the fans what your team values are and the strategy for moving forward.

'I have always been open and honest with the media and they have been kind to me over the years because of it.'

MICHAEL CLARKE

FIELDING TIPS

WATCH THE SEAM

My Australian teammate Mark Waugh was the best slip fieldsman I have ever seen, and I was amazed how easily it came to him. His 181 catches in Test cricket, mostly from second slip, is in the top five of all time.

Firstly, his stance at slip was strong, yet relaxed, feet shoulder-width apart and the fingers pointing down. Mark always watched the bowler deliver the ball and looked for the length of the delivery, then watched the rotation of the ball flying past the batsman. This is massively important, and it is worth noting for all slippers.

Mark always said if the batsman nicked the ball and the seam of the ball was scrambled, then the ball was not travelling quickly and was likely to dip at the last minute. Sometimes when a batsman nicked the ball, the seam would be spinning like Saturn, horizontally or even vertically, which told him that it was travelling 'hot', or very quickly.

So by watching the rotation of the ball, a slip fieldsman can tell exactly how quickly the ball is travelling to him.

THE RIGHT WAY TO CATCH

In Australia, we have always been taught to have ten fingers up or ten fingers down when attempting to catch. It is standard practice, and you cannot be caught between those two positions. But I have noticed that over the last 15 years or so some of the best slip fieldsmen, like Mark Waugh, Ricky Ponting, Mahela Jayawardene, Shane Warne, and Mark Taylor, used a few variations on this.

The modern way to catch is to overlap your hands, assuming that you have put two hands on the ball, with the dominant or throwing hand in front to take most of the force of the ball. There is very little diving involved; great slip fieldsmen don't need to dive, as they have great balance.

If you look at any decent wicketkeeper's gloves, you will see that it will have wear marks on the dominant, or throwing hand of that player. So slip fieldsmen are now copying the keepers in the way they catch, in my opinion. This overlapping technique stops the ball from bursting through their hands when the ball is coming through with speed.

Interestingly, Ricky Ponting loved catching the ball in slips with ten fingers up. Scientific studies using special glasses proved that Ponting was watching the bottom of the ball when it flew to him, and thus caught mostly with ten fingers up. Everyone is different, and Ponting surely was

Many players now use gloves at practice, with the fingers cut out to alleviate any chance of bruising. The Australians, who have probably been the best fieldsmen over the last 20 years, love to have their fielding practice and catching at full throttle, with no easy catches. They take just as much pride in their fielding skills as their batting or bowling.

If you have lost some confidence in catching, try catching a seven-kilogram shot putt. If a slipper or fieldsman catches, say, ten shot putts from two metres, then tries to catch a cricket ball, it gives him the feeling of catching a tennis ball, *because it is* so much lighter. Try it, and you will see that it is good for confidence.

MARK WAUGH

WHERE TO LOOK

When you are fielding, it is a personal decision as to where you watch. Is it the ball that you are following, or do you look at the batsman on strike? We have just noted that Mark Waugh, for instance, liked to look at the ball in flight, but not everyone is the same.

I have asked many players over the years which method they favour. If it is the bat that they watch, which part of the bat? A lot of them say that in slips they watch the edge of the bat, but which part of the edge? Personally, I like to keep the game simple, so I would watch the ball at all times.

But even then there can be confusion. If you are fielding at mid-on, should you watch the ball? There are many different answers. Two of the greatest fieldsmen that I have ever seen in Sir Vivian Richards of the West Indies and Mark Waugh of Australia both told me that they watched the ball all the time, no matter where they were fielding.

I was watching Viv closely at Adelaide once when he was fielding in the covers, and I could not believe how quickly he moved to the ball. It was as though he was one step ahead of the batsman. I asked him later over a beer what was his theory, and he answered: 'Deano maan, I watch "Mako" (a faster bowler, the late, great Malcolm Marshall) release the ball. I look for his length. Maan, if I see it short, I move towards point straight away. If he bowls length, I hold my position. Maan, but I was deathly smooth to maintain balance ... you know so I could pick up the ball. You know, Deano, I don't dive coz I don't have to, maan ...' He finished with a belly laugh in that West Indian way.

They don't come any better than Viv Richards, so I recommend that you try it. Just as you would when you are batting, watch for the bowler's length, maintain your balance, and don't be scared. My mantra is that the ball can hurt you ... but not the bat! You catch the ball, not the bat.

FIELD OF DREAMS: VVS LAXMAN

Most of the great teams field well, *really* well, which includes not just the catching but the ground fielding and the ability to hit the stumps. Bad teams downplay fielding, and I know that when I was playing for Australia, we never allowed it to be secondary. VVS Laxman had some thoughts about this, and he was one of the great slips catchers that I have seen. VVS reckoned his whole game rode off his fielding.

'I always thought, if you caught well, you batted well,' he told me. 'I took my fielding very seriously, and I am proud to say I took one catch per Test, which works out to be 135 Test catches in my career.

'I loved fielding at second slip. Very early in my career, Rahul Dravid and I had the great opportunity of talking about slip catching with the ex-Australian coach Bobby Simpson, and he told us that our feet should not be much wider than shoulder-width apart, and that our knees and weight should be on the INSIDE of our feet. This allowed us every opportunity to go after the ball if it came to us low or high. Both of our results in catching improved dramatically after that!

'I know the great Australian slippers Mark Taylor and Mark Waugh would have contests over who would take the most catches in a series, and Rahul Dravid and I were no different. We trained hard together, and we always wanted to take 100 catches a day, to improve our skills and confidence. I know 100 catches is a lot, but if you want to be the best, you have to put in the work.

'If our hands were sore, we wore gloves. Actually, we often wore gloves for the new balls, to protect our knuckles from being bruised and battered — a little trick that we learned from the former New Zealand captain Stephen Fleming back in the early 1990s. New Zealand can be a very cold place, and it's hard to field in slips with cold hands, trying to catch new balls!

'I recommend that you try to love your fielding as much as your batting and bowling. Just note when selecting teams, the first thing that irritates selectors is the fact a player is not good at fielding. It's about pride in your performance and putting the work in.'

VVS LAXMAN WORE GLOVES AT FIELDING PRACTICE FOR PROTECTION

GENERAL TIPS

PRACTISE EARLY: MICHAEL CLARKE

Michael Clarke, the former Australian captain, told me that he liked to get to a ground before everyone else in his teams. The reason: he wanted to complete all his extra training before the team came, so that he could join in the full-team routines, having already done his 'extras'. 'Sure, I would do slip catching and warm-ups together, but I wanted to be around the younger players helping their own preparations for a Test or ODI match,' he told me. 'I loved the adage of, "What can I do to help you today?" I think the players always enjoyed that I was there if they wanted me.

'Also, I had to be available for press and other duties, like welcoming or introducing special VIP guests or sick children into the team environment. I really loved players getting their Australian caps on their debuts. Why other clubs and teams don't do it is beyond me — having a past great talk about why the cap was so special to them and how it changed their lives. Many players tear up; it is a very emotional moment for everyone.'

MEDIA PERSPECTIVE: HARSHA BHOGLE

Dealing with media can be tough for a player, especially if he is having a rough trot, and many players get distracted by this. They find it hard to handle, and they react badly to criticism or the most minor questioning of their position. Ultimately, it is a negative on their game, I found.

I got on well with the media through my career, but I asked the Indian broadcaster Harsha Bhogle for a perspective on this. He believes players can develop a siege mentality.

'I tell a lot of young players: "Nobody in the media can stop you from scoring a run or taking a wicket or taking a catch. So don't let them come in your way",' he told me.

'Some sportsmen and sportswomen have a tendency to feel that the media is about tearing them down. Some feel there is a personal agenda against them, which in most cases is not the case at all.

'The media is there for a reason, and if used wisely, they can help you really connect to your fans and supporters. Being a public figure like a cricketer, the fans will always love you irrationally. Yes, be humble and be positive in the way you present yourself to the media, but

HARSHA BHOGLE

tell us something we don't know about you or the day's play, something interesting that the media might not have picked up on.

'I have always loved this quote from the writer Rudyard Kipling: "If you can meet with Triumph and Disaster. And treat those two impostors just the same ..."

'So remember, when facing the media through bad form or through triumph, the fans will always support you if you are honest and interesting. You don't have to tell them everything, but if you are interesting, it's amazing how the media will always support you along with your fans.

'Just remember these points: keep things simple and interesting, score runs, and take wickets. Respect the media and the job that they do and don't carry an attitude or a superior air, and all things will work out for you, in Disaster or in Triumph!'

THE RIGHT WAY TO PRACTISE (1)

It makes me so angry when I see teams practising before a match with the obligatory six guys in a semi-circle throwing the ball to a batsman three metres away, waiting for a catch. They were doing this when WG Grace was playing, and many teams still do it! It is no wonder some guys hate practising.

We have to move with the times, and what captains must do is to organise more one-on-one practice. For instance, one batsman and one fielder taking catches, so six groups of two where the batsman is hitting a lot of balls. Now, this drill shows me two things: for one, just how good the bat planes are of each batsman if he can hit the ball back to the fieldsman consistently; and two, the skills of the fieldsman as to whether he is catching the ball correctly or not.

How I can tell if a fieldsman is watching the ball into his hands is whether I can see the button on top of his cap, commonly referred to as the squatchee, when the ball goes into his hands. When I watch great wicketkeepers like Rodney Marsh, Ian Healy, Adam Gilchrist, and Brad Haddin, I can always see the squatchee on their cap when they take the ball properly.

Not only does this drill improve players' catching, it also improves bat planes on batsmen. Simply, you cannot hit the ball straight, consistently if the batsmen's bat plane is poor.

My pre-game practice depended on how strong my form was. If I was in good nick, I would do about 20 throwdowns with a lot of catching and fielding. If I was not in good form, I would have long practice sessions until I felt right. If I was facing a lot of left-arm fast bowlers, I would ask guys to bowl around the wicket. If I was facing the West Indians, I would be asking guys to bowl off less than 20 metres to simulate the pace that I was about to encounter in the middle.

MERV HUGHES

THE RIGHT WAY TO PRACTISE (2)

I was into training as hard as I could. Hit your catches as hard as you could, do everything at full pace. Long skill training sessions are ridiculous; do it properly, then do something else, I say. But it can come undone at times!

I remember one day in Perth, I asked big Merv Hughes, my teammate, to bounce me in the nets because I had just came back from India where the pitches turned and were slow. I knew that I needed to get onto the back foot more often, but Merv declined my request because he knew that the WACA Ground practice pitches had a tendency to be dangerous. They are also very fast.

I said: 'Merv, just do as you're bloody told!' So he said ,'Okay', and I can remember thinking that the big fellow did not like to be told what to do. I was actually expecting a fast yorker to try to knock my toes off! But Merv followed his instructions, and let go with a ferocious bouncer that hit the badge on my helmet.

I slumped into semi-unconsciousness, and as Merv picked me up, he told me: 'I told you I would kill you!' I never asked Merv to bounce me again.

EQUIPMENT: BAT WEIGHT

Trust me when I say this, if you want to hit it big, it is not about the size or weight of the bat, it is about your hand speed. Interestingly, most of the biggest sixes that have been hit on grounds around the world were struck by the old bats and not by the big, new-style bats that are made today. For example, my old teammate Simon O'Donnell hit a couple of the biggest sixes at MCG and SCG, Mark Waugh hit one onto the roof of the grandstand at the WACA Ground, and Kim Hughes hit one into the top deck of the members' pavilion at Lord's with the old-style bats. These guys had great hand speed, which

gave them the energy needed to hit the ball miles.

With bat weight, the easiest bit of advice I can offer is to pick up the bat with your non-preferred hand — in my case, my left — and raise the bat with a straight arm to shoulder level. If the bat is slightly shaking under the pressure, then the bat is too heavy for you.

I have always thought that the handle is the most important part of the bat. Indian-manufactured bats have a tendency to be a little tight, and I always loosened them up before I hit a ball.

Sure, it's nice to have eight grains across a blade, but my best bat had only four, with a knot on the bottom of the blade. I never used my playing bat for practice.

Hardly any professional batsmen use oiled bats anymore. They always place tape on the front of the bat for protection and are basically too lazy to oil them, as they get all their bats for free.

If a bat feels no good after a few hits, change the grip or put some tape under it. If it still feels poor, that bat can be used for firewood. Bats today rarely need breaking in. Use them and smash them, I say.

EQUIPMENT: GLOVES AND PADS

Throughout one calendar year I would go through a minimum of 50 pairs of gloves and six pairs of pads. My batting gloves were made very specifically to my own needs. Firstly, they would be cut to my own hand size, and secondly, the leather of the palm was made very thin, more like a golf glove. Lastly, to break them in, I would put them on and punch the hell out of the wall like a boxer punching a punching bag.

After that, I would wash my hands, as there would be a talc powder on my hands, and put my wet hands in the gloves and do it all again. This would take me ten minutes.

With my batting pads, I would pull the velcro tabs as tightly as I could and jump all over them. I would break the cane in the bottom to widen the entry where my boot would fit. I also placed another bit of foam in my front pad, as the pads still didn't absorb the shock when a Malcolm Marshall hit you.

In the old days, I heard that England Test cricketer Derek Randall would ask his wife to wear his new pads while she did the housework. I don't think that would work for most cricketers today!

THE T20 EXPERIENCE

I have talked about the importance of defence in batting and in bowling, too. Now with the prominence of and demand for T20 cricket, the defence in this form of the game is the bowler's ability to bowl defensive lines and lengths, and the fielding skills of your team.

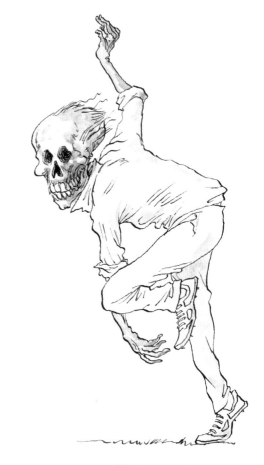

THE DEATH BOWLER

Firstly, when I sit down and select my T20 team, the rationale that I follow is:

1. Who are my death bowlers? I want to get wickets in the Powerplay overs, but I also want my death bowlers to do a job.

2. The next important players are my top-three batsmen. These guys have to smash it straight away and be able to hit boundaries at the death (overs 17–20).

3. The next player I select is a high-quality spinner. The best T20 spinners are bowlers who can spin it both ways now. Off spinners are being found out, now that they cannot bowl the doosra, so they had better learn to churn out a good 'arm' ball for the variation.

4. The next guys are my 'bangers', or power-hitters. Now, I want my guys to score at a strike rate of 150 plus, or 150 runs per 100 balls faced. My banger must be able to bowl, too. The best banger in the world, the one I would pick first, is Andre Russell of the West Indies, but other notables would include Kieron Pollard, also West Indian, or even MS Dhoni, the Indian veteran who is one of the great finishers of all time.

THE TOP THREE BATSMEN

THE SPINNER

T20: WHERE IT IS WON AND LOST

Where T20 games are mainly won and lost is in the ability of your death bowlers to hit correct defensive lines and lengths and whether they are properly supported by fieldsmen doing their job in the field.

The proper defensive lines and lengths are these:

1. Yorker *landing* two feet (0.6 metres) outside off stump
2. Yorker aimed at middle and leg stump
3. Change-up slower-ball bouncer.

If you don't have these skills, you will be smashed by batsmen today. Take a look at what happened in the last over of the 2016 T20 World Cup final between England and the West Indies. English bowler Ben Stokes was bowling to Carlos Brathwaite, where the West Indies required 24 to win. Stokes continued to bowl good-length balls, which we would call 'slot' balls. Brathwaite was able to get under them and hit four sixes to win the final. There was not one yorker or slower bouncer, and Stokes paid a heavy price on a big stage.

Fielding is everything in T20 cricket. Firstly, the captain must place his best fieldsmen in what we call 'hot spots', where the ball continues to travel. The T20 game is so exciting and good to watch, with batsmen hitting the ball all over the place and the fieldsmen always trying to throw down the stumps.

What I must say as a NON-NEGOTIABLE is that when the ball is hit into the deep on the off side, all boundary riders on the leg side must run into the circle to back up poor throws from deep. This game is about defence and not offence, contrary to popular opinion. In general, great bowling teams defeat great batting teams, and a great example of this was the Indian Premier League 9 when Sunrisers Hyderabad defeated the talented Royal Challenge Bangalore team, which had Virat Kohli, Chris Gayle, AB de Villiers, and Shane Watson.

THE BANGER

HAVING MENTORS

I believe you cannot chase your dreams with any success unless you have quality people around you, people whose opinions you value and respect, and people who respect you. I had two mentors in my life: my dad and Keith Stackpole.

I was so lucky to have a dad like I did. My father, Barney, was captain and coach for many years for Carlton Cricket Club in Melbourne, Victoria, in the District competition that was just one step below first-class cricket. He was there for me through thick and thin. He never threw me a ball, but was there for me when times were tough.

It was great to have someone to bounce ideas off and give me the confidence to find my best. Dad passed away some 15 years ago now and he was my best friend. I miss him terribly.

My technical mentor, if you like to call it that, was Keith Stackpole, who was a past vice-captain of Australia and who captained Victoria. He was also captain of the Carlton Cricket Club when I arrived there at 13 years of age.

Right from an early age, 'Stacky' worked on my technique and how to practise properly. I copied his ruthless attitude when it came to batting. He was attacking against the quicks and was a beautiful stroke player. Right throughout my years as a professional player, Stacky would ring up and give me advice on my technique or attitudes that needed to be fixed. He was always there for me, and his influence on me was huge.

All players are recipients of copious amounts of information from coaches, friends, and teammates, and it needs to be filtered. The key is to speak to your mentor first, so that you can work out which pieces of advice actually help your game, and which parts are rubbish. Because there is plenty of that offered.

A cricketer who reaches the pinnacle will go through maybe a dozen coaches through the levels, all with their own philosophies and ideas about how to play the game. A player can get lost in information, which is why mentors are so critically important.

BARNEY JONES, DEANO, AND KEITH STACKPOLE